Christmas
Lights Up Brazil

Christmas Lights Up Brazil

Christmas Around the World
From World Book

World Book, Inc.
Chicago

Staff

Executive Committee

President
   Jim O'Rourke
Vice President and Editor in Chief
   Paul A. Kobasa
Vice President, Finance
   Donald D. Keller
Vice President, Marketing
   Jean Lin
Vice President, International
   Maksim Rutenberg
Vice President, Technology
   Jason Dole
Director, Human Resources
   Bev Ecker

Editorial

Senior Manager, Database Content
   (regions/sciences)
   Mike Schuldt
Senior Researcher
   Lynn Durbin
Administrative Assistant
   Ethel Matthews
Manager, Contracts & Compliance
   (Rights & Permissions)
   Loranne K. Shields

Graphics and Design

Senior Art Director
   Tom Evans
Senior Visual Communications Designer
   Melanie Bender
Senior Designer
   Isaiah Sheppard
Coordinator, Design Development
   and Production
   Brenda Tropinski
Senior Cartographer
   John M. Rejba
Media Researcher
   Rosalia Bledsoe

Manufacturing/Production

Manufacturing Manager
   Anne Fritzinger
Production Specialist
   Curley Hunter
Proofreader
   Nathalie Strassheim

Marketing

Director, Direct Marketing
   Mark R. Willy
Marketing Analyst
   Zofia Kulik
Digital Marketing Coordinator
   Anisha Eckert

World Book, Inc.
180 North LaSalle Street
Suite 900
Chicago, Illinois 60601 USA

© 2018 World Book, Inc. All rights reserved. This volume may not be reproduced in whole or in part in any form without written permission from the publisher.

WORLD BOOK and the GLOBE DEVICE are registered trademarks or trademarks of World Book, Inc.

Library of Congress Cataloging-in-Publication Data for this volume has been applied for.

Christmas Lights Up Brazil
ISBN: 978-0-7166-0835-6

World Book wishes to thank the following individuals for their contributions to this book: Rosalia Bledsoe, Leonard Durbin, Jacqueline Jasek, Emily Kline, and Donna Ramlow.

A previous version of this book was published with the title *Christmas in Brazil*. World Book also wishes to thank all those who contributed to that publication, including Rebecca A. Lauer, Kathryn Blatt, Dirce Guerra Bottallo, Fabio Bottallo, Marilúcia Bottallo, Astrid Cabral, Alvaro Marins de Almeida, Selma Monroe, Nilson C. Nas Cimento, Ariani B. Friedl, Liana Pérola Schipper, and Braulio Tavares.

For information on other World Book publications, call 1-800-WORLDBK (967-5325), or visit our website at www.worldbook.com. For information on sales to schools and libraries, call 1-800-975-3250 (United States), or 1-800-837-5365 (Canada).

Printed in China by Shenzhen Donnelley Printing Co., Ltd.,
Guangdong Province
1st printing September 2017

Previous spread and table of contents: A church in Gramado, Brazil, at Christmastime. In Brazil, both Christmas lights and summer flowers herald the arrival of the holiday season.

Contents

6 Christmas Comes to Brazil
16 Light and Drama
24 Sharing and Preparing
32 Christmas with Family
46 Welcoming the New Year
56 More Music and Celebration
67 Crafts
71 Recipes
77 Carols

Fireworks light up the sky above a giant Christmas tree floating on a platform in the Rodrigo de Freitas Lagoon in the Brazilian city of Rio de Janeiro.

Christmas Comes to Brazil

In a city square, wide-eyed children gaze with wonder at the brilliant lights of a giant Christmas tree. At an oceanfront beach, a million merrymakers cheer while fireworks burst and twinkle on New Year's Eve. The Christmas season in Brazil is a kaleidoscopic whirl of dazzling light displays and big, colorful parties.

Light also illuminates treasured family time on Christmas Eve and Christmas Day. A grandmother's eyes glow with joy when children and grandchildren arrive for Christmas Eve dinner. Later that night, thousands of candles flicker as churches throughout the country welcome people to midnight worship services.

Christmas in Brazil—like the nation itself—blends the traditions of many diverse people. It is a busy season of preparation and celebration. It is also a special time for sharing the peace and quiet blessings of Christmas with family and friends.

For many people, the word *Christmas* brings to mind images of frosty mornings, sleigh bells, and children watching for winter's first snowflakes. For children in Brazil, however, the excitement of Christmas arrives in the sunny days at the start of summer vacation—the school year in this South American country starts in February and ends in mid-December.

Celebrating Christmas in a tropical land

Brazil is a large country that covers nearly half of South America. The equator runs through the far northern part of Brazil, so most of the country is in the Southern Hemisphere, where

Christmas Lights Up Brazil

City lights show off Rio de Janeiro's dramatic setting between forested hills and the shining waters of the Atlantic Ocean. Brazilians sometimes call Rio Cidade Maravilhosa, *which means* Marvelous City.

summer starts in December and ends in March. The climate is generally warm. Since summer temperatures range from about 70 °F (21 °C) to more than 100 °F (38 °C), the Christmas shoppers crowding the streets wear shorts and T-shirts. A family may celebrate Christmas Day with a barbecue, a pig roast, or a day at the beach. Yet one person still dresses as if for a snowy winter. *Papai Noel,* which means *Father Christmas,* is the name that Brazilians have given to Santa Claus. In spite of the heat, Papai Noel wears the traditional fur-trimmed red suit, big black boots, and long white beard when he visits Brazil.

Portuguese colonists brought Christianity and the celebration of Christmas to Brazil when they began to settle there about 500 years ago. Even today, Portuguese Christmas traditions re-

Christmas Comes to Brazil 9

The Portuguese navigator Pedro Álvares Cabral (top) claimed Brazil for Portugal in 1500. In 1822, Prince Pedro of Portugal (shown below, being cheered by Brazilians) proclaimed the nation independent.

main at the heart of Brazil's holiday customs. As in Portugal, for example, going to church for midnight Mass is an essential part of the celebration for many Brazilians.

Gradually, however, Brazil's environment lent new dimensions to old European traditions. Churches sometimes conducted their midnight Mass outdoors in the warm summer night. Cooks began to flavor holiday treats with tropical fruits. Today, turkey—a bird native to America—is a favorite main course at Christmas dinners.

A people with many roots

Today's Brazilians are proud to be a people with many roots. The unique richness of their Christmas celebrations has come from the combined influences of many different cultures.

Before the Portuguese arrived, an estimated two to five million South American Indians from many different groups lived as hunters and farmers in what is now Brazil. Anthropologists believe the ancient ancestors of these people came to the Americas thousands

Brazil covers nearly half of South America and has about as many people as all the other nations on the continent combined.

The Land of Brazil

Brazil is the fifth largest nation in the world in both physical size and population. In northern Brazil, the mighty Amazon River winds through the world's biggest tropical rain forest, which covers half of the country. More than 40,000 varieties of plants grow there. Parrots, toucans, and over 1,500 other kinds of birds fly through the trees.

Although the rain forest is probably the region most people picture when they think of Brazil, this huge country also has other types of land. All along its incredible 4,600 miles (7,400 kilometers) of Atlantic coastline, fabulous beaches and fine harbors attract thousands of tourists every year. Most of the population lives within 200 miles (320 kilometers) of the ocean. The largest cities, such as São Paulo and Rio de Janeiro, are coastal cities in the south. The Northeast—the area that bulges out into the Atlantic Ocean—includes a dry interior region called the Sertão, where cactuses grow. Wetlands lie in the Pantanal at the western border of central Brazil. South of the Sertão, interior highlands and plateaus provide the nation's best farming and ranching land.

Christmas Comes to Brazil 11

> Christ the Redeemer, one of the world's largest and most famous statues, stands on Corcovado Mountain overlooking Rio. The statue depicts Jesus Christ with arms outstretched, as if embracing the faithful.

of years ago by crossing a land bridge that existed then between Asia and what is now Alaska and also, possibly, by crossing from far northern Asia to America in small, coastal-hugging boats. *Indigenous* (native) peoples are the true, original Brazilians. Today, they make up about one percent of the population. Their foods and customs have continued to influence the nation's overall culture.

In 1500, the Portuguese explorer Pedro Álvares Cabral landed on the east coast of Brazil and claimed it for Portugal. Portuguese colonists began to settle the region during the 1530's. The name *Brazil* came from the word *pau-brasil,* the Portuguese name for the native brazilnut tree. Today, Portuguese is the nation's official language. When Brazilians wish each other Merry Christmas, they say it in Portuguese, "Feliz Natal" (*fay LEESH nah TOW*).

Some Portuguese colonists established large sugar plantations in northeastern Brazil. At first they tried to use Native Americans to work their plantations, but soon they began to bring Africans to Brazil as slave laborers. Today, the African influence on Brazilian culture remains strongest in the northeastern regions, such as Bahia.

Gradually, the Roman Catholic religion also became central to the lives of most African Brazilians. In Salvador, the capital of Bahia, the

Samba musicians show off their flair in the streets of Brazil. Samba, the most famous style of Brazilian music, developed from rural Afro-Brazilian dance music. Its syncopated rhythm became popular in the nation's cities during the early 1900's.

graceful Church of Nossa Senhora do Rosário dos Pretos stands as tribute to the devotion of African Brazilians, some of them slaves, who built the church in the 1700's. They decided to build a church of their own when they were not allowed to worship together with Europeans. Today, many aspects of Brazil's holiday celebrations reflect a blend of African and European influences. The country's tradition of boisterous holiday parades, for example, combines African traditions of celebration through music and dance with a medieval European custom of lively religious plays and processions.

Brazil became independent of Portugal during the 1800's. The path to independence began in 1807, when France invaded Portugal and the Portuguese royal family fled to Brazil. The king returned to Portugal in 1821, leaving his son Pedro behind to rule Brazil. Pedro declared Brazil independent in 1822 and was

Christmas Comes to Brazil

Visitors who come to Natal for Christmas events also find themselves drawn to the area's beautiful, palm-lined beaches.

A Town Called Christmas

On January 6, 1598, the Portuguese established a fort near the easternmost point of South America's Atlantic coast. January 6 is Epiphany, the day when the Roman Catholic Church celebrates the visit of the Wise Men (also called Magi) who brought gifts to the baby Jesus. The Portuguese called their new fort the Forte dos Reis Magos (Fortress of the Magi Kings). The fort is shaped like a star, a common defensive design at the time. Nevertheless, the shape is particularly appropriate for a fort named after the Wise Men, who followed a star to Bethlehem.

On December 25, 1599, the Portuguese founded a village near the fort and named it *Natal,* the Portuguese word for *Christmas.* Today, Natal is the capital of the Brazilian state of Rio Grande do Norte.

Naturally, Christmas is a big deal in a city named after it. Natal hosts Christmas concerts, plays, and decoration contests. In early December, its *Carnatal* is a multiday celebration with music and dance. Carnatal is similar to Carnival—the spectacular festival before Lent for which Brazil is famous.

soon crowned as its emperor. In 1889, imperial rule ended and the nation became a republic.

Over the centuries, the dominant Portuguese population in Brazil has intermarried with the country's African and indigenous peoples to create a distinctly unique national character. Since the 1800's, immigrants from Germany, Italy, Japan, Poland, and other lands also have added to the ethnic mix. Christmas customs also reflect their influences, with German gingerbread figures, for example, showing up as holiday decorations and even as characters in Christmas parades. Today, Brazil is one of the largest "melting pots" in the world. The nation has a population of about 200 million people distributed over a far-reaching and varied landscape.

Christmas today

Brazilians delight in the diverse, yet shared, traditions that make up their colorful Christmas celebrations. Many public holiday events are dramatic and exciting. Cities blaze with Christmas lights. Crowds gather for flashy parades, as well as holiday concerts and plays. Fireworks and lavish parties welcome the New Year. Yet, for most people, the celebration of Christmas Day itself remains a private time of family togetherness.

Christmas is one of the holiest days of the year in Brazil. On Christmas Eve, most families gather for a big dinner. Many people also attend a midnight Mass or church service, where they listen to the age-old story of the coming of Christ, the meaning of Christmas, and the need for universal peace and brotherhood. After church is over and the children have gone to bed, the adults stay up drinking coffee, enjoying conversation, or joining in music and song. Brazilians are renowned for their lively, free-spirited, and colorful celebrations. Merrymaking will continue over the next few weeks, especially on New Year's Eve. But meanwhile, Christmas is a special holiday—the birthday of the infant Jesus. This holy day is celebrated in true Brazilian style, with singing and possibly some dancing as well. If the festivities last all night long—that's Christmas in Brazil!

Christmas stars beckon to visitors at this park in Belo Horizonte, capital of the southwestern state of Minas Gerais.

Light and Drama

From the northern port of *Belém* (a name that means *Bethlehem* in Portuguese) to the southern city of Pôrto Alegre, Brazilian towns greet the Christmas season with brilliant lights and colors. Beautifully decorated trees appear in city squares. Light exhibits somehow grow more imaginative every year. There are seasonal plays and performances. Some towns even transform themselves into Christmas villages. For children, however, one of the biggest events is the appearance of a very special visitor—Papai Noel.

17

Like people in Europe and North America, Brazilians start preparing for Christmas well in advance of the holiday. Signs of the season appear in November, when store windows and town streets are dressed with Christmas decorations. Many cities also sponsor free Christmas shows and concerts.

In a country where Roman Catholicism predominates, the religious aspect of Christmas is very strong. Nowhere is this more apparent than in the Nativity scenes—called *presépios (pray ZEHP ee oos)* in Portuguese—that people set up in their churches and homes. The Nativity scenes in Brazil's great cathedrals and churches often have life-sized images of Jesus, the Virgin Mary, and Joseph. As angels soar above, shepherds and Wise Men approach the humble stable. The presépios are so splendid that everyone wants to go to church to see them.

City lights

At night, cities glow with Christmas lights. Brasília, constructed in the 1950's to encourage the development of Brazil's interior,

Windows—and rooftops—announce that Christmas is just around the corner. No doubt the choirboys looking out from these windows will want to perform at their best.

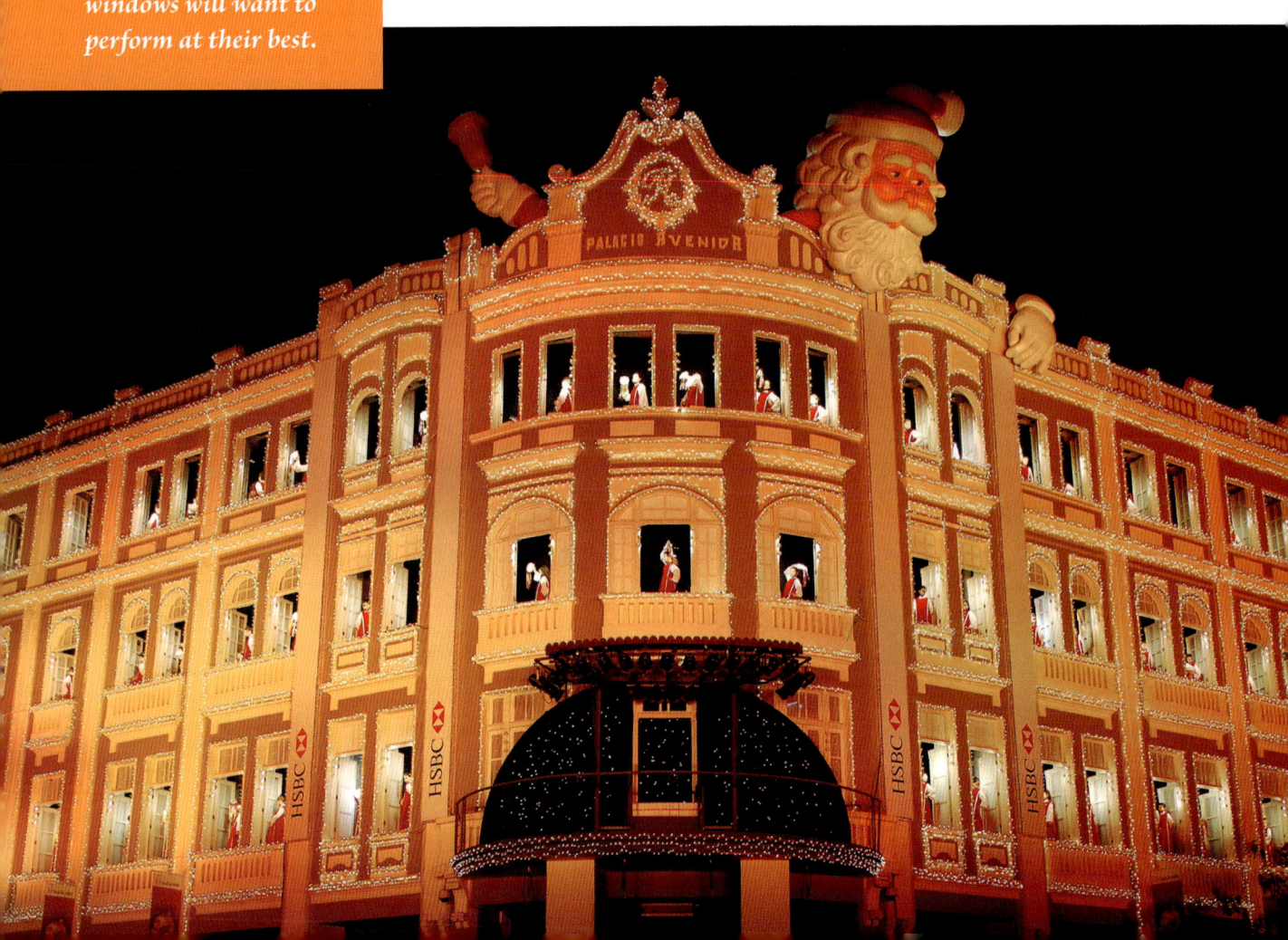

In towns across the country, crowds gather to watch tree lighting ceremonies at the start of the Christmas season. This tree stands in Ibirapuera Park, the largest public park in São Paulo, the largest city in Brazil.

officially became the nation's capital in 1960. For the Christmas season, the city has been known to light the dramatic arches of the Juscelino Kubitschek Bridge across Lake Paranoà in holiday colors. Other towns also illuminate bridges and streets with sparkling snowflakes, graceful angels, and other Christmas images. The coastal city of Recife has even reflected light images off a screen of water droplets sprayed by pumps into the air above the Capibaribe River.

For many Brazilian towns, the holiday centerpiece is a giant Christmas tree in the town square. These are not usually real trees. Many are light displays—a metal frame covered by lights or a cone-shaped screen lit from inside. The theme of the decorations often changes from year to year. One year, a tree twinkles with musical notes and instruments. Another year, the lights form stars and angels or nutcrackers and gingerbread figures. On some trees, lights shift from image to image as the viewer watches. The trees make popular backdrops for family photographs to send in Christmas cards. Although most trees stand in city squares, Rio de Janeiro has had a giant tree that floated on Rodrigo de Freitas Lagoon.

Light and Drama 19

During this performance on the lake in Gramado, the singers stand on island platforms around a gold-lit fountain, while fireworks flare overhead. The city's Christmas festival is appropriately called Natal Luz, *which means Christmas Lights.*

Christmas towns

Magical toys dance. Acrobats dressed as snowflakes twirl through the air. Papai Noel takes a bow, as fireworks light up the sky. From November to January, the towns of Gramado and Canela in mountainous resort areas of southern Brazil turn into Christmas wonderlands, as they host hugely popular Christmas festivals.

Actors, singers, dancers, and musicians present daily parades and shows. Some plays tell magical stories of Christmas dreams or toys come to life. Others present the story of the first Christmas. In Gramado, a small lake provides the setting for a floating stage, and the water reflects the colors and light of the performances. In Canela, the beautiful Cathedral of Our Lady of Lourdes provides the backdrop for religious dramas and choir concerts. Both towns also have Christmas shops, and children may visit Papai Noel.

Christmas Lights Up Brazil

Nativity plays

Another impressive custom in Brazil is the *Auto de Natal* (Nativity play), which tells the story of the birth of Jesus. The tradition of the *auto*—an entertaining one-act religious play—dates back to Europe in the Middle Ages. In America, Portuguese missionaries used such plays to teach Bible stories to the Native Americans. Often the plays are staged outdoors. In a holiday tourist center, such as Canela, the Auto de Natal may be a major theatrical and musical event. In other places, it might be a simpler production, perhaps staged in front of the local church. One popular location in Rio de Janeiro is a large outdoor theater in front of the dramatic arches of the Arcos da Lapa, the remnant of an aqueduct built in the 1700's to carry water into the city. The play has a devoted following and draws a large crowd.

Many Brazilian children participate in school Nativity plays. These amateur dramas bring the age-old story of Mary, Joseph, and Jesus alive for children and parents alike. Not only do the children enjoy dressing up as these important people, but parents and teachers also find it is a great way to teach young people about the true meaning of Christmas.

Proud children take part in a Nativity performance at the Basilica of the National Shrine of Our Lady of Aparecida, near the city of São Paulo. Meanwhile, proud parents record the event on their phones.

He's here! Papai Noel touches down in a helicopter to bring Christmas greetings to children and parents.

Here comes Papai Noel

For kids, one of the most spectacular events of mid-December is the arrival of Papai Noel. Tradition says Papai Noel comes all the way from his home in Greenland, and his arrival in Brazil is a major event. His first local appearance of the season might be at a welcoming ceremony in a shopping mall. Sometimes he rolls into town with a parade. When it comes to Papai Noel, you never know where he might turn up—or how he'll arrive.

In Rio de Janeiro, the special event has even taken place in Maracanã Stadium, the city's largest sports stadium. Thousands of children and parents gathered to watch and wait. Papai Noel was definitely on his way— but not in a sleigh pulled by reindeer. This time, he came by helicopter! After touching down in the middle of a colorful landing pad, he waved and wished everyone "Boas Festas" ("Happy Holidays"). The children shouted and cheered. Then, it was time for a sing-along. Led by Papai Noel and well-known singers, the stadium swelled with the sound of Christmas carols, popular Brazilian tunes, and favorite children's songs.

Whether in a big city or a small town, the arrival of Papai Noel draws people from miles around. Children look forward to it every year. Many of them will remember the fun for years to come.

Brazil's Beautiful Game

For some people outside of Brazil, Maracanã Stadium might be familiar as the location of the opening and closing ceremonies of the 2016 Summer Olympic Games, which were hosted by Brazil. However, Brazilians originally built the giant stadium more than 60 years earlier for their favorite sport—soccer.

In Brazil, soccer is called *futebol* (FOOCH eh bohl), the Portuguese word meaning *football*. First introduced to the country in 1894, the game spread like wildfire. Brazilians play all year long—in school, in clubs, on sandy beaches, and in city parks. Experts have compared the Brazilian style of play to the grace and skill of a dance. Watching professional futebol is a national passion in a country that loves *o jogo bonito* (the beautiful game). Businesses have even been known to close down for World Cup finals. Brazil won its first World Cup in 1958. In 2002, it became the first nation ever to win five times.

Brazilians love to play soccer anytime and anywhere—even barefoot at the beach.

Light and Drama

Christmas is a time for giving. These volunteers carry supplies to help low-income families in a rural part of the country.

Sharing and Preparing

As Christmas trees appear in town squares and twinkling lights brighten the streets, Brazilian families start preparing for Christmas, too. Everyone searches for just the right present to buy or card to send. Families unpack treasured decorations. There are gifts to share and the fun of secret surprises.

Sharing with others

Christmas is the season for giving and, like others who celebrate the holiday throughout the world, Brazilians go Christmas shopping for their friends and family. The search for the right gift starts in earnest at the beginning of December. No one wants to wait until the last moment.

Often, gifts are not extravagant. A family of modest means may buy their children basic necessities like shoes and clothing. Those who are more comfortable also might surprise their children with books, dolls, or video games.

A law known as the "13th salary" helps make Christmas a little more affordable for everyone. This law ensures that every Brazilian worker receives an extra month's pay each year. Workers generally chose to receive half of their 13th salary earlier in the year, often in the month when they take their vacation, and to get the other half in December as a "Christmas bonus." Introduced in the early 1960's, the popular 13th salary gives people a little extra money for Christmas gifts and celebrations. It is a welcome addition to the family income.

Papai Noel brings gifts to these children living in Maré, a favela in northern Rio. Favelas are crowded shantytowns that have grown up around many major South American cities, as millions of poor rural people have moved to urban areas seeking a better life.

Many Brazilians generously share their blessings at this time of year by giving to the poor and underprivileged. The Roman Catholic Church sponsors many fund-raising events at Christmas, often in conjunction with Protestant congregations or other church organizations. This unity is especially appropriate, since Christmas Day in Brazil is considered a day of spiritual union among churches.

People from all walks of life attend bingo games and raffles to raise money for toys and gifts. Everyone seems to enjoy these affairs, which often take place outdoors. The atmosphere frequently resembles that of a festival, with an abundance of flowers, music, and flags. Some organizers distribute gifts right on the spot. In other cases, the money raised provides Christmas dinner and gifts to make the season brighter for families who need assistance.

Another custom is to bring a small gift, wrapped simply in white, to church on Christmas Eve or on another designated Sunday in December. The church then distributes the anonymous gifts to people in need.

Preparing at home

Christmas in Brazil wouldn't be Christmas without the presépio—one of the most important of all Brazilian traditions. Since the Nativity scene represents Christ's birth, it receives a place of honor in each home.

Some presépios are heirlooms that have been in the family for generations. It is not unusual for a Brazilian family to have a presépio that belonged to a great-grandmother or even a great-great-grandmother.

In some cases, the Nativity scene may be so large that it fills a whole room. Other presépios are small and simple. Most fall somewhere in between and would fit on a coffee table, carefully placed on the mother's finest embroidered tablecloth. Many families set up the presépio near their Christmas tree.

Presépios always include Mary, Joseph, and the baby Jesus. Usually, they also include shepherds and Wise Men. Perhaps

there is an angel, a star, cows, and sheep. And, of course, there is a rooster. The Brazilian custom of placing a rooster in the Nativity scene stems from an old tradition that says a rooster crowed to announce the birth of the Christ Child on the very first Christmas.

Each family member is free to add his or her own personal touch to the basic scene. Young boys may decide to surround Jesus and the shepherds with an electric train. Girls may add a toy swan or a sailboat.

Many animals and plants native to Brazil find their way into the Nativity scene. Maybe an alligator is trying to sneak up on the sheep. A mysterious Amazonian jaguar crouches behind a rock. Pineapples, bananas, and red mangoes sit on desert sand or even inside the manger with the baby Jesus. Never mind that these tropical fruits had never been seen in Bethlehem at the time of Christ's birth. For Brazilians, they make the presépio

Presépios come in many shapes and sizes. Some, like these, stand outdoors. Their designs and materials are as varied as each artist's imagination, but all of them share the message of joy at the birth of the Christ Child.

more colorful and interesting. The end result is a Nativity scene that blends the old and the new, the innovative and the traditional. Brazilians don't mind the anachronisms. Instead, it is as if they are offering up all of nature and human achievement to the Holy Child, incorporating both past and present.

Some Brazilians assemble a handmade presépio each year using everyday household items. They may shape mountains out of papier-mâché or even paper bags. A mirror serves as a lake. A china goose on the mirror creates an interesting reflection. Small pieces of fresh plants turn into trees and shrubs. Especially ambitious crafters create new figures of the Holy Family, perhaps painted or dressed in doll clothes, every year.

Many Brazilian presépios are works of art—beautifully arranged, with every detail in place. Still others may look somewhat comical, because no two figures are the same size—the baby Jesus towers over his parents, or a sheep is larger than a camel. These details don't matter. Creating the presépio is a national pastime, and if everyone has a good time making the Nativity scene, that's what counts.

As the days get closer to Christmas, Brazilians also start to think about putting up their Christmas trees. Most families have an artificial tree, especially in the more tropical regions where traditional fir trees don't grow. Decorations range from neon-bright metallic ornaments to beautifully handmade clay figurines. An angel often tops the tree. Fresh tropical flowers and bright red poinsettias, which grow wild in Brazil's climate, add color to the house.

Schoolchildren decorate a classroom Christmas tree on Combo Island in the rain forest region of northern Brazil.

Sharing and Preparing

The lucky recipient of this Christmas basket can feast on sausages, fruit, cheese, chocolate, and champagne.

Even though the weather is warm and balmy, the decorations often suggest a traditional white Christmas. Puffs of white cotton beneath the tree and on its branches make it look like snow has fallen.

Friends and secrets

At this time of year, Brazilians busily write and send Christmas cards to friends and acquaintances. True to the typical European Christmas, many of the cards show winter scenes. Papai Noel with his reindeer may glide across a snowy landscape. Many cards picture Christmas trees covered with snowflakes or children bundled up in warm clothing, even though these scenes do not reflect Christmas in Brazil. This custom has been changing, however. It is now possible to find Christmas cards that show palm trees on sandy beaches or Christmas trees without snow.

Many Brazilians treat family, friends, or employees to a *cesta de Natal*, or Christmas basket, filled with all sorts of food. They also use the baskets to thank mail carriers, hairdressers, and others who provide services. Brazilians stuff these colorful, festive baskets with practically every kind of food and drink required for a scrumptious Christmas feast. Some baskets contain fine wine or champagne and irresistible chocolates, nuts, and sweets. In others, dried fruits and canned goods nestle under the colorful cellophane wrapping. A cesta de Natal may be big or small. The baskets come in every price range, and almost everyone can find something affordable.

One of Brazil's most popular gift-giving customs is called *Amigo Secreto,* or Secret Friend. A group of friends, co-workers, schoolchildren, or family members write their names on pieces of paper and put them in a bowl. Then everyone draws a name. No one reveals the identity of his or her secret friend. It's strictly confidential. The players each buy something for the person whose name they drew. When people open their gifts on Christmas Eve, they find out who drew their names. However, office workers may open their gifts together a few days before Christmas, and schoolchildren may exchange gifts before school closes for summer vacation.

Sometimes, the Amigo Secreto gifts are "gag" gifts. Everyone competes to find the most outrageous present. Often, the gift obviously does not suit the receiver, such as baby clothes for a six-foot-tall man or a toy cell phone for a teen who is always texting. Everyone has a good time laughing along with the person who gets the funniest gift. Sometimes there are two rounds of giving—the first with gag gifts, the second with regular ones.

The busy December days rush past. Families look forward to getting together, and the cooks pull out favorite old recipes. Preparing for the Christmas Eve feast usually means buying a turkey for Christmas dinner. By then, Christmas Eve may be only a couple of days away. Soon it will be time to open presents. Soon everyone will get together with friends and family. Relatives may be driving from distant regions to spend the holiday with the family. All will enjoy the huge Christmas feast. This is one of the most eagerly awaited times of the year, especially for the children. Christmas will soon be here.

Christmas is a time for family—and Papai Noel, of course!

Christmas with Family

It's the night before Christmas and… No one is tucked up asleep in this house!

The children race after a soccer ball in the yard. Father helps Grandfather Carlos check to see that everything is ready for a barbecue at the beach tomorrow. Uncle Jorge, dressed in the red suit and white beard of Papai Noel, mops his brow in the summer heat and prepares to surprise the kids with presents. He pauses to adjust the figure of Joseph—the one he himself once played with as a child— in the Nativity scene on a table by the Christmas tree. In the kitchen, he sees Grandmother Luiza check on the turkey in the oven—the family will need plenty of time to eat before they leave for midnight Mass. But first, it is time for a very special visit.

Christmas Eve in Brazil is very much a family affair. It's a time when relatives get together to share Christmas dinner, called the *ceia de Natal (SAY yah djee nah TOW)* in Portuguese. Married children with their own brood of kids converge on the house of their parents, so that grandparents and grandchildren can celebrate together.

For most Brazilians, December 24th is a very busy day. Everyone takes part in the preparations. If the family has not set up its presépio yet, the father may start early and work all day to get it ready. Some parents even follow an old tradition of waiting until the evening of Christmas Eve to put up the family's Christmas tree. Meanwhile, the house gets a last minute sprucing up. The children lay out the new clothes that they will wear to Christmas dinner and the midnight church service. Usually, the mother has the awesome responsibility of cooking the dinner—no small task by anyone's standards.

Ceia de Natal

Many Brazilians enjoy cooking, and they start preparing the Christmas feast early on Christmas Eve. Many years ago, Brazilians generally followed Portuguese tradition and served dried cod as the main course at Christmas. Although some people still opt for cod, roast turkey is now the favorite main dish. Other common choices are pork roast and ham. A big gathering might feature them all.

Brazilians stuff their turkeys with a special *farofa (fah ROH fah)* dressing, which is different from the kind of dressing served in Europe and America. Farofa consists of coarse manioc flour toasted in a heavy frying pan with butter and other ingredients. Manioc flour comes from the starchy, potato-like root of a small shrub known by several names—cassava, manioc, or yuca. The Native American people in Brazil used starch from manioc roots to make small cakes long before the Portuguese arrived. Today, Brazilians eat farofa as a side dish and sprinkle it over soups and stews. In stuffing, they use it in place of bread crumbs. Other common ingredients include turkey liver, turkey

> Rabanada (above) is a traditional dessert on Christmas Eve, but this display looks almost too good to eat. Bolinho de bacalhau (below) are deep-fried codfish balls. Fish, especially cod, was a traditional Christmas food in Portugal.

gizzard, onions, garlic, hard-boiled eggs, olives, and bacon.

Dried cod continues to make an appearance in many Christmas Eve dinners as a sort of fish cake known as *bolinho de bacalhau (boh LEEN yah djee bah kahl YOW)*. Cooks dice the cod and mix it with mashed potatoes, onions, sweet peppers, tomatoes, and olives. They shape the mixture into balls that they then deep fry.

Christmas Eve dinner also includes all sorts of side dishes and desserts. *Arroz (ahr ROHSH)* is white rice, often cooked with onions, nuts, raisins, and a variety of other ingredients. Okra, shredded kale, and other vegetables may be on the menu. The table always features platters of fresh tropical fruit—pineapple, mangoes, bananas, and more. In addition, grapes are especially popular at Christmastime.

No Christmas feast would be complete without a dessert called *rabanada*. Rabanada is very similar to French toast and is so well-loved that it has become a national institution. In addition

Christmas with Family

to the friendly competition that exists among home cooks, there have even been formal contests to see who can make the best rabanada.

Brazilians make rabanada from loaves of French bread. They purchase the bread ahead of time and leave it out all night to make it slightly dry and stale. They soak each slice of bread in milk, dip it in beaten eggs, and fry it to a golden brown. Then, they cover the warm slices with cinnamon sugar. Sometimes, they also drizzle the bread with syrup made of port wine, honey, and cinnamon. Rabanada is delicious and easy to prepare—small wonder it's a favorite throughout the land.

Other popular desserts at a traditional Christmas feast include cookies, mousse, custards, and ice cream. Some family recipes have been handed down through the generations. These desserts may be known only as "Grandma's cake" or "Maria's pudding," named for the person who originated the recipe.

In a country as vast as Brazil, many variations on the Christmas celebration exist. Individual families with different ancestries have preserved different customs and foods, although some ethnic traditions have merged together or spread throughout the population. For example, custards were a popular Portuguese dessert. Brazilians continue this passion, but often add tropical ingredients, such as coconut or passion fruit. Italian immigrants, who began arriving in

In late December, both bakeries and home bakers are busy making tall, fruity panettone for holiday dinners.

Christmas Lights Up Brazil

As dusk falls on a balmy Christmas Eve, a family pauses to admire their neighbors' decorations before dropping in to wish them "Feliz Natal."

large numbers during the late 1800's, enjoyed panettone—a holiday bread with almonds, raisins, and orange peel. Now, nearly all Brazilians look forward to this seasonal treat.

Christmas parties usually feature all sorts of nuts. Early Portuguese settlers wanted to celebrate Christmas with foods that reminded them of home, so they imported walnuts and chestnuts from Europe. Roasted chestnuts remain a part of Christmas Eve celebrations, joined by native nuts, such as cashews and Brazil nuts. Families often set out nuts and other snacks in the early evening for visitors who may drop by. Besides, Christmas dinner won't be served until 10 o'clock or later, so everyone needs a little something to nibble until it's time for the big meal.

Christmas visitors

In some communities, young people traditionally go door-to-door around 6 or 7 o'clock in the evening to wish their neighbors "Feliz Natal." People invite the merry wanderers in to celebrate

Christmas with Family

the holiday with coffee, cookies, nuts, and wine. The atmosphere is warm and festive, and it's a good time to share the spirit of Christmas with neighbors. Shortly after 7 o'clock, the well-wishers head home to be with their immediate families.

Some families enjoy playing games during the evening or singing Christmas songs around the tree. *"Noite Feliz"* (*"Silent Night"*) and *"Boas Festas"* (*"Happy Holidays"*) are among the favorites. *"Boas Festas,"* a song written by Brazilian composer Assis Valente, tells how poor children feel during the Christmas season. Many children sing this tune:

*Anoiteceu, o sino gemeu, a
gente ficou feliz a rezar...
eu pensai que todo
mundo fosse filho de Papai
Noel...*

(The night has fallen, the
bells are tolling, and we were
happy as we prayed.
I used to think that everyone was Papai Noel's child.)

Christmas Eve is also a time when Papai Noel makes house calls. Some parents hire people to dress up as Papai Noel and visit their children, while other parents enlist friends or relatives for the job. In any event, it is a wondrous experience for the children—here is Papai Noel in person, come just to visit them! They can actually talk to him, sit on his lap, and tell him how well behaved they have been. More often than not, Papai Noel brings a huge sack full of gifts—and that is the best part of all! Out of the sack, he pulls toys and games, books and clothes. Children in Brazil attack their presents like children do everywhere—with great enthusiasm and no restraint whatsoever. Some especially perceptive young people may recognize the gift-giver behind the beard and realize that this Papai Noel is really their next-door neighbor or their uncle, but no matter. He brings presents and a jolly spirit, and Christmas just wouldn't be Christmas without him.

In some regions, however, it is not the custom for Papai Noel to make an actual appearance. Instead, families may put the children's presents outside the door and pretend that Papai Noel left them there. Around midnight, the children find and open their brightly wrapped gifts.

In other cases, the children carefully place their shoes near a window or under the Christmas tree. The shoes will be filled with gifts when the children awaken in the morning. The Brazilian version of Santa Claus does not come down the chimney, however. Papai Noel slips the gifts in through the window or simply walks in the front door.

Still another custom is for parents to hide presents outdoors. The children search for their gifts—much as children hunt for Easter eggs in America and other countries. Since the weather is warm in Brazil and there is no snow, Christmas gifts can be hidden outside without them getting wet or ruined.

It looks as though Papai Noel found these shoes tucked beneath the Christmas tree and left the child who owns them a treat of nuts and oranges.

Missa do Galo

Christmas dinner and midnight Mass are two of the most universally practiced Christmas customs in Brazil. Many people eat Christmas dinner around 10 or 11 o'clock at night and then go to a midnight church service. Since about two-thirds of the people are Roman Catholics, this is most often a midnight Mass. Protestant churches in Brazil also have well-attended Christmas services—more than a fifth of the people are Protestant Christians. Some families go to church first and then have their Christmas dinner, which makes for a very late night indeed.

The midnight Christmas service is one of the holiest church services of the year. Incense and fragrant flowers scent the air. Adults and children join in singing hymns and saying prayers aloud.

The beautifully illuminated Cathedral of Our Lady of Lourdes in Canela welcomes worshippers to Christmas midnight Mass.

There are readings from the Scripture and a Christmas sermon. Many people receive Holy Communion in remembrance of Christ's Last Supper. In some churches, people leave gifts for the poor in front of the presépio. The children and adults sing as they proceed down the aisle, leaving their presents next to the Holy Child. In this way, they observe one of the basic teachings of Christmas—that it is more blessed to give than to receive.

The origins of a Christmas midnight Mass are uncertain but

Christmas Lights Up Brazil

probably date back to about the A.D. 400's. Roman Catholic popes eventually established the practice of celebrating three Christmas Masses—the first at midnight, for the hour of Jesus's birth; the second at daybreak, for the shepherds' veneration; and the third, called the Mass of the Divine Word, later on Christmas Day. The midnight Mass is sometimes called the Mass of the Rooster—*Missa do Galo* in Portuguese. This name probably stems from an old legend about the animals present when Jesus was born. The legend said that the rooster crowed to give the world the first sign of the Christ Child's birth.

While many Brazilians attend the Missa do Galo, some prefer to watch a Christmas service on television at home. In recent years, this custom has grown increasingly popular in the large coastal cities, such as Rio de Janeiro and São Paulo. The Vatican broadcasts the midnight Mass offered by the Pope all over the world, and Brazilians are not the only people tuning in. Some Protestant churches in Brazil also televise their Christmas worship services.

After church, many families simply go home to bed. The chil-

During this midnight Mass, children carrying flowers stand near the priest as he holds an image of the Christ Child.

Family members enjoy visiting over well-crafted cups of coffee.

dren put out their shoes for Papai Noel before going to sleep. For families who attended church before sitting down for their Christmas dinner, however, it's finally time for the long-awaited ceia de Natal. Even children stay up for this late, late meal.

Some families celebrate all night long. Adults may drink *cafezinho (kah fay ZEEN yoh)*—tiny cups of strong coffee, whose name means *little coffees*—to help them stay awake. Along with wine and cafezinho, there is a constant flow of lively, light-hearted conversation. Relatives from different cities have a lot of catching up to do. The warm weather often draws people outdoors, where they may sit and converse for hours on the backyard patio. Finally, in the wee hours of the morning, everyone says good night and drifts off to sleep at last. Tomorrow is, after all, Christmas DAY. It will be a good time to relax and unwind.

Christmas Day

Excitement rules on Christmas morning for children who did not open their gifts on Christmas Eve. Some of them find presents right beside their bed. Other children discover gifts in the shoes they left near a window or under the Christmas tree. Now they have new toys to play with and new clothes to wear.

People who did not attend a midnight Mass or church service may go to an early Christmas morning service instead. For most Brazilians, Christmas Day itself is fairly quiet and subdued. Everyone has the day off from work and school, and this in itself makes Christmas Day enjoyable. Many young people living along the coast spend the day at the beach. Others just meet with friends to enjoy the national holiday.

Often relatives and friends gather for a big lunch of leftovers from last night's Christmas Eve dinner. Barbecues are also popular on Christmas Day. Everyone dresses casually in shorts and T-shirts. They set up a huge picnic table outside. Once the grill is hot, they cook skewers of beef, chicken, pork, and sausage over coals or an open fire. Some ambitious cooks dig a pit in their backyard and have a pig roast.

The men usually do the barbecuing, while the women prepare the side dishes. The meal includes potato salad and plenty of tropical fruit. The weather is ideal for a barbecue, hot and sunny, and the party lasts most of the day.

At last, Christmas Day draws to a close, and it is time to go home and get some rest—but not for long. Christmas may be over, but the Christmas season is still in full swing. From December 24 through January 6, Three Kings' Day, activity continues almost nonstop. Various religious festivals mark the end of the year, but the most dazzling event is the New Year's Eve celebration. While Christmas is a quiet and family-centered event, most of the New Year's festivities are colorful, frenzied, loud, and exuberant. Brazilians like nothing better than to set work aside and take part in a festival, and now, in the middle of the summer and the Christmas season, that's exactly what they do.

Crowds flock to the beach on a hot Christmas Day. The beach is one of the most popular places to spend the holiday relaxing with family and friends.

Christmas with Family

Flavors of Brazil

Brazilian food is a melting pot of flavors. It combines mainly Portuguese, African, and Native South American ingredients and cooking methods to create a uniquely Brazilian cuisine. Brazilians have come up with some unusual foods, such as manioc fries and piranha broth. However, not all their dishes would be unfamiliar to North Americans. Pizza and hamburgers are big favorites.

Brazilian cooking uses three kinds of flour—wheat, corn, and manioc. The Portuguese settlers who came to America wanted to continue cooking with the wheat flour they had been accustomed to back home, but they eventually had to start using American ingredients, too. Native Americans ground corn into flour. The indigenous peoples of the Amazon region also cooked with starch extracted from manioc (also known as cassava) roots.

Fast food, Brazilian style. Many street vendors, especially in Bahia, sell acarajé (ah kah rah ZHEH)—delicious patties of ground black-eyed peas and shrimp, deep-fried in dendê oil.

Sometimes, the Portuguese found ways to incorporate these new ingredients into their own familiar recipes—such as making cakes with corn meal.

The Africans brought to Brazil as slaves in colonial times also found ways to pre-

Brazil nuts come from one of the tallest trees in the Amazon rain forest. The trees can get up to 150 feet (46 meters) high. They produce heavy, woody fruits that look similar to coconuts. Each contains about 12 to 24 nuts. Standing under one of these trees can be dangerous when the large fruit falls from a lofty treetop.

It's a guy thing. Traditionally, men have done the barbecuing. Fathers and uncles taught sons and nephews their family's own special way of seasoning meat, positioning it over the coals, and turning it until it reached slow-grilled perfection.

serve the familiar tastes of home whenever they could. For example, they added *dendê (DAHN djeh)* oil, a cooking oil obtained from the red fruit of the African oil palm, to *moquecas (moo KEH kahs*—stews) and other foods. The palm grows well in Brazil. Dendê oil is a common ingredient in Brazilian cooking, particularly in Bahia, the region where African cultural influences have remained the strongest.

Thanks to a long Atlantic coastline and the huge Amazon River system in the north, seafood is a big part of the Brazilian diet. Soups and stews made with fish, shrimp, and other seafoods are common in the Amazon and coastal regions. Cooks often simmer the stews in a coconut milk sauce and serve them over rice. Brazilians eat rice and beans nearly every day.

Brazil is famous for its cattle ranches and quality beef. The gauchos on the ranches of the arid Sertão region shredded up dried beef and mixed it with beans, rice, and farofa. The people of this region called dried beef *carne-de-sol*, meaning *beef of the sun*.

The gauchos of the Sertão and southern Brazil barbecued large pieces of beef on long skewers. They stuck one end of the skewer in the ground and leaned it over an open fire, turning the skewers periodically to roast all sides evenly. Brazilian barbecue, called *churrasco (chu RAHS koh)*, is very popular in both homes and restaurants.

Since the 1800's, new immigrant groups have added more twists to the Brazilian diet. Italians developed a wine industry in the country's southern highlands. Japanese sushi has become popular in the nation's cities.

The warm climate provides a year-round array of fresh vegetables and tropical fruits that show up in salads, desserts, main dishes, and cooling drinks. One of Brazil's most popular soft drinks is made from the guaraná, a berry with a high caffeine level that grows in the Amazon region.

Christmas with Family

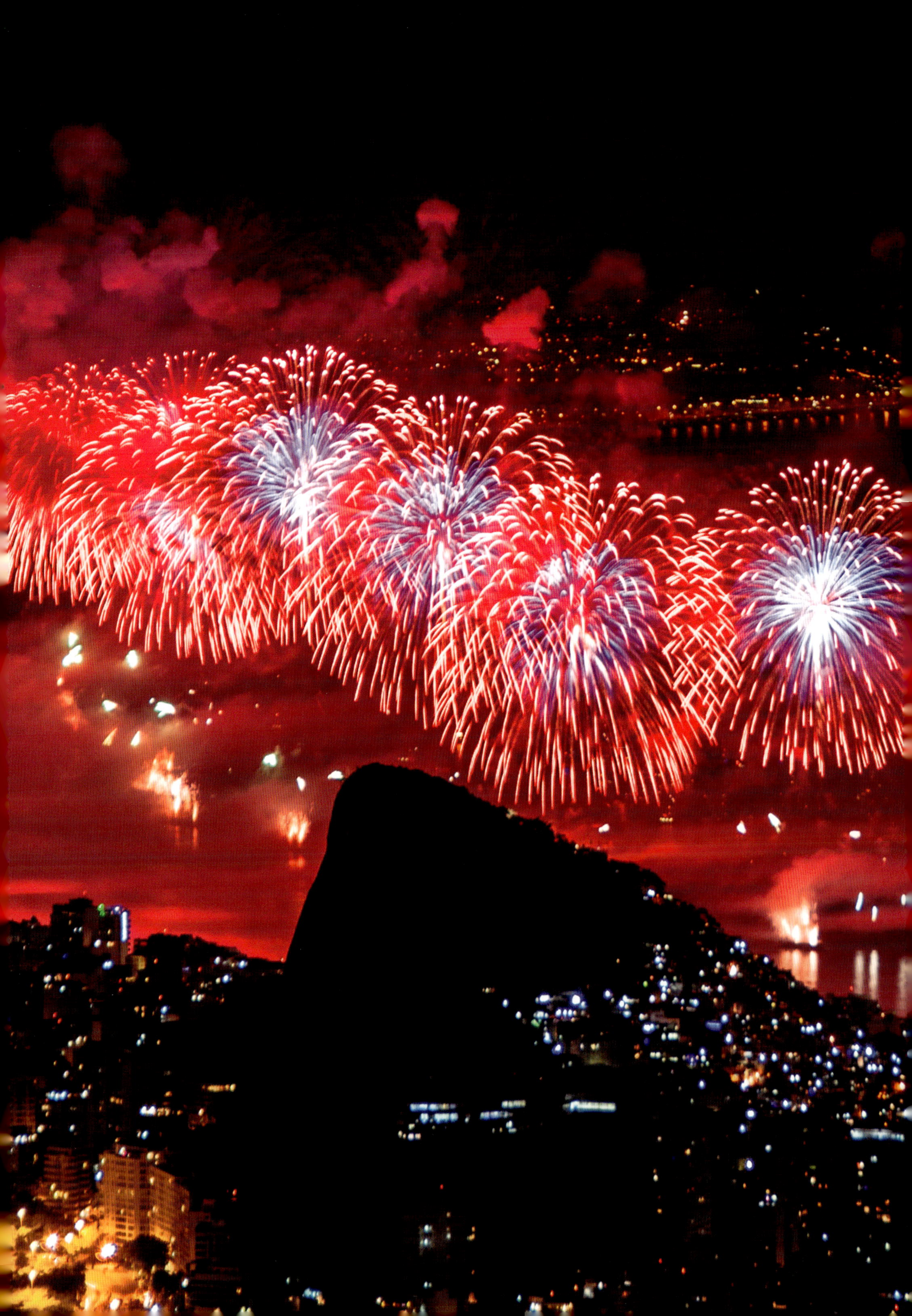

Rio's Copacabana Beach is one of the best places to watch the city's world-famous New Year's Eve fireworks display.

Welcoming the New Year

Brazilians call New Year's Eve *Réveillon (reh vay YOHN)*, a name that comes from the French word *réveiller,* meaning *to awaken. Réveillon,* as the term is used in Brazil, means *to awaken the new year*—and Brazilians set out to do just that.

While Christmas in Brazil is a private and holy occasion, people usher in the New Year with a loud, public, and spectacular bang in a colorful mixture of American, European, and African celebrations. The city of São Paulo stages an international marathon with a cast of thousands, while Rio de Janeiro offers a shoreline festival in honor of Iemanjá *(ee ah mahn DJAH),* an African goddess of the sea. Throughout the country, Brazilians greet the New Year with spectacular fireworks and all-night celebrations. There is truly something for everyone.

47

Racing into the new year

A thousand nervous kids stretch, jump, and jog in place on a warm day in mid-December. These young runners, ages 6 to 16, are warming up for the races of the São Silvestrinha (Little Saint Silvester). The event takes place every year at a large stadium in São Paulo. It includes races of different lengths and for different age groups. The younger children run mostly for fun, but the older teens compete seriously for medals.

The São Silvestrinha began in 1993. It is an offshoot of the Corrida Internacional de São Silvestre (Saint Silvester's International Road Race), an international marathon held every year on New Year's Eve.

The adult marathon takes place in downtown São Paulo and attracts thousands of participants. It starts and ends on Avenida Paulista, São Paulo's main avenue. The circular route stretches 15 kilometers, or slightly more than 9 miles. The distance is almost twice the original length of the race when it began in 1924.

On the morning of December 31, thousands of people eagerly gather to run or to support the athletes. Some participants have prepared for weeks or even months—rising in the early dawn and running each day to get in shape for the marathon. Many have devoted every spare moment to jogging and exercising so that they will have the stamina to go the entire distance. Still others are professional runners who have traveled far to compete in the event.

Friends and relatives turn out in droves to watch their runners and cheer them on. Avenida Paulista is awash in a sea of people. The city has blocked off the streets along the race's route to accommodate the crowd. The runners stand out in their bright-colored shorts, tank tops, and professional running shoes. The energy level mounts as starting time draws near.

Finally, a signal sends the runners off with a joyful roar. Like horses penned up too long, they bolt from the starting point. They forge through the city streets, while the crowd, caught up in the excitement, shouts encouragement. Great athletes from around the world jog next to normally sedentary business peo-

From near and far, crowds of athletes gather on the morning of New Year's Eve to run the São Silvestre marathon through the streets of São Paulo.

ple. When the race is over, awards go to the first man and the first woman to finish the race and to the runners-up.

Over the years, the adult competition has undergone a number of changes. Originally, it started at the stroke of midnight on New Year's Eve. Eventually, the race became a popular televised event, with millions of viewers watching it at home. Organizers thought that more viewers would be able to watch if the race took place in the daytime, and indeed, this has been the case. At first, they moved the event to the afternoon, but Brazil's daytime summer heat was hard on the athletes. Today, the marathon begins during the morning on New Year's Eve. The new scheduling allows people to enjoy the race during the day and take part in nighttime festivities, too.

Seaside celebrations

Nowhere in Brazil are the celebrations of New Year's Eve more flamboyant, rambunctious, and just plain awe-inspiring than

Welcoming the New Year

49

on Copacabana Beach in Rio de Janeiro. The city enjoys one of the most spectacular geographical settings in the world. It lies on beautiful Guanabara Bay, rimmed by sandy beaches and lagoons. Forested mountains rise to the north and west. Rio has more than 50 miles (80 kilometers) of beaches, including the world-famous Copacabana and Ipanema, names synonymous with sun and surf. Dominating the landscape, the famous cone-shaped Sugar Loaf Mountain rises from a peninsula in the bay. On New Year's Eve, Rio's beaches come alive with open-air concerts and many parties.

Amid all this natural beauty, the people of Rio also hold one of the nation's largest and most distinctly Brazilian celebrations—the Festival of Iemanjá. The festival is an African spiritualist ceremony that honors Iemanjá, the goddess or queen of the sea.

Brazil is home to several African spiritualist religions, such as Candomblé and Umbanda, that developed in South America mainly from African religious traditions. Followers believe that divine beings called *orixás* (also spelled *orishas*) serve as links with a higher god, and that orixás and the spirits of the dead can communicate with the living through individuals called *mediums*. In colonial times, some of the African slaves in Brazil began to associate individual African orixás with particular Catholic saints. For example, ideas about Iemanjá became intertwined with devotion to the Virgin Mary, so pictures of Iemanjá often depict her much like Mary, dressed in a white gown with a blue robe draped over her head. Some Brazilians who consider themselves to be Catholics also participate to some extent in rituals traditionally associated with African spiritualism.

Early in the morning on December 31, thousands of people gather along the shore at Copacabana and some other beaches to honor Iemanjá. For believers, it is a time to thank her for the blessings of the past year and to ask for good will in the upcoming twelve months. Many people who do not subscribe to African spiritualism nevertheless turn out for this unusual and beautiful celebration, which lasts until dawn the next day.

This image of Iemanjá, dressed in blue, wears a crown as queen of the sea.

Women carry a little blue boat filled with flowers, a gift for the queen of the sea (above). At the water's edge, a celebrant dressed all in white spreads her arms and welcomes the New Year (left).

Celebrants carry candles and flowers to the beach. Many of the women wear billowing white skirts adorned with ruffles and lace and wrap white turbans around their heads. They often add flowers as necklaces or to adorn their hair. Sometimes the person actually performing the ritual dresses in blue.

As night falls, participants place thousands of white candles in the sand, turning the famous crescent-shaped beach into a shimmering carpet of light. Drums begin to roll. Believers dance, sing, and convulse when, according to myth, Iemanjá enters their bodies and possesses them.

Believers and nonbelievers alike may pay tribute to Iemanjá

Welcoming the New Year

by bringing gifts. Iemanjá is a vain creature, who likes to receive jewelry, mirrors, flowers, and money. At the stroke of midnight, thousands of people run into the ocean, clothes and all, carrying their presents. Some simply toss their gifts into the foamy waters, while others cast them forth in little wooden boats. According to legend, if your gift floats out to sea, Iemanjá finds it acceptable and you will have a good year. If your gift washes ashore, it is not a good sign, and the following year will not be happy. Usually, the waves wash all the gifts out to sea.

With great exhuberance, everyone tries to jump over seven waves. According to tradition, you can ask Iemanjá for a favor or make a wish for each wave you jump. To some this may seem to be sheer superstition, but to others it is lots of fun and just might bring good luck and prosperity in the coming year. It's hard to resist the raw energy and joy of the event.

As if all this were not enough, the night sky, usually peaceful, suddenly roars from its slumber with the sounds and lights of a hundred fireworks. To everyone's delight, the big hotels along Copacabana Beach compete with one another to see who can put on the most impressive New Year's Eve display. The end result is a fabulous evening of bursting, brilliant fireworks. The dancing and music continue long into the night. Some of the celebrants do not leave the beaches until early dawn.

Awakening the New Year

There is much to do on New Year's Eve in Brazil—many parties to attend and activities to enjoy. No one gets much sleep this night, and why should they? Réveillon is about awakening a new year. If the New Year was ever asleep, it surely will be awake by the time Brazilians finish celebrating.

At large parties throughout the country, musicians play popular Brazilian music and people toot on party horns. As the traditional New Year's Eve countdown begins, the crowd falls silent. When the clock strikes midnight, custom dictates that every woman greet a man before she greets another woman. The same holds true for the men—they must greet a woman before

A cruise ship in the harbor is a great place for watching the New Year's Eve fireworks. From shore, the ship itself, strung with lights, becomes part of the sparkling scene.

they acknowledge another man. The custom is supposed to ensure that each person will be lucky in love.

Afterward, everyone welcomes the New Year with loud shouts of laughter and joy. People throw themselves into each other's arms, hugging and kissing and wishing each other "Feliz Ano Novo," which means "Happy New Year." Spectacular fireworks can be seen—and heard—outside. Church bells ring in the New Year, and shrill blasts from car horns and sirens add to the joyful din. From every direction, Roman candles shoot high into the sky, firecrackers bang, and brilliant flares light up the night. The singing and dancing continue until the wee hours of the dawn—and not till then does anyone even consider going home. After all, it is the Réveillon, and everyone loves the party.

Tradition claims that eating a portion of lentils exactly at midnight on New Year's Eve ensures prosperity for the upcoming year, so lentils often appear on New Year's Eve menus and buffet tables. Wearing white clothing is another New Year's Eve

Welcoming the New Year   53

The Brazilian samba dancer Selminha Sorriso performs here on a beachfront stage during a New Year's Eve concert.

custom. The color symbolizes peace, hope, and renewal. A dash of accent color can represent a wish for a particular type of luck—perhaps gold for money or red for love.

In the cities, some people attend spectacular balls and formal parties hosted by large hotels and nightclubs. Couples dance until dawn to the rhythmic beat of the *samba* and *lambada*. The samba is the national music of Brazil, while the lambada developed later, but both remain popular. Beach concerts and parties explode with still newer Brazilian styles that blend samba with rock, reggae, and strong African rhythms.

The majority of people, however, forgo the elaborate New Year's affairs and choose something more informal. Often, they simply get together at a friend's house for a small, casual party. These impromptu gatherings, which start around 8 or 9 o'clock in the evening, are no less festive than the grandest celebrations in the best hotels. Of course, there is plenty of food and music. Perhaps the festivities grow lively when one person strums a guitar or starts humming a song. Another partygoer "just happened" to arrive with a *rabeca* (rah BAY kah—Brazilian fiddle). A few guests may add to the beat with whatever is on hand—beans shaken in a jar or forks tapped against glasses and plates. The music gets the party going, and the infectious rhythm of a samba proves irresistible. Soon, everyone starts singing and dancing. Shyness is the one thing that is frowned upon, and no one is allowed to sit on the sidelines.

As midnight draws near, the group may move to the beach. With a fire built on the sand and blankets spread out, the partygoers munch on snacks. Somebody pours the champagne, and everybody waits for the fireworks to start. This is a simple yet beautiful way to celebrate the Réveillon—under the stars at the ocean's edge. While only those living along the coast can spend New Year's Eve on the beach, Brazilians everywhere enjoy fireworks displays in local parks or fields.

Sand Castles Instead of Snowmen

During the Christmas holiday season, children in northern countries ice skate and build snowmen. Brazilian kids are more likely to visit a beach and build sand castles. Brazil is famous for the beautiful beaches that line much of its long Atlantic coast. For both Brazilians and tourists, the beaches promise great fun in the sun.

In coastal cities, beaches act as meeting and gathering places. Exercise groups work out there in the mornings. Families spend a day in the sand with their kids. Office workers walk over during lunch or even hold meetings on the beach. Many city dwellers relax with a stroll or a bicycle ride along the water at the end of the day. In the evening, parties liven up the scene with music and dancing. Beaches are sometimes the setting for live musical concerts. On New Year's Eve, many towns launch fireworks over the water as people watch from the shore.

Food stalls (above) are a great place to grab a snack—perhaps a pastel (pahs TOW—meat and vegetable filling in a deep-fried crust), or a churro (deep-fried pastry stick). The stalls also serve soft drinks, beer, and fresh fruit and coconut drinks. During the Christmas season, you might see a sand statue of Papai Noel at the beach (below).

Welcoming the New Year

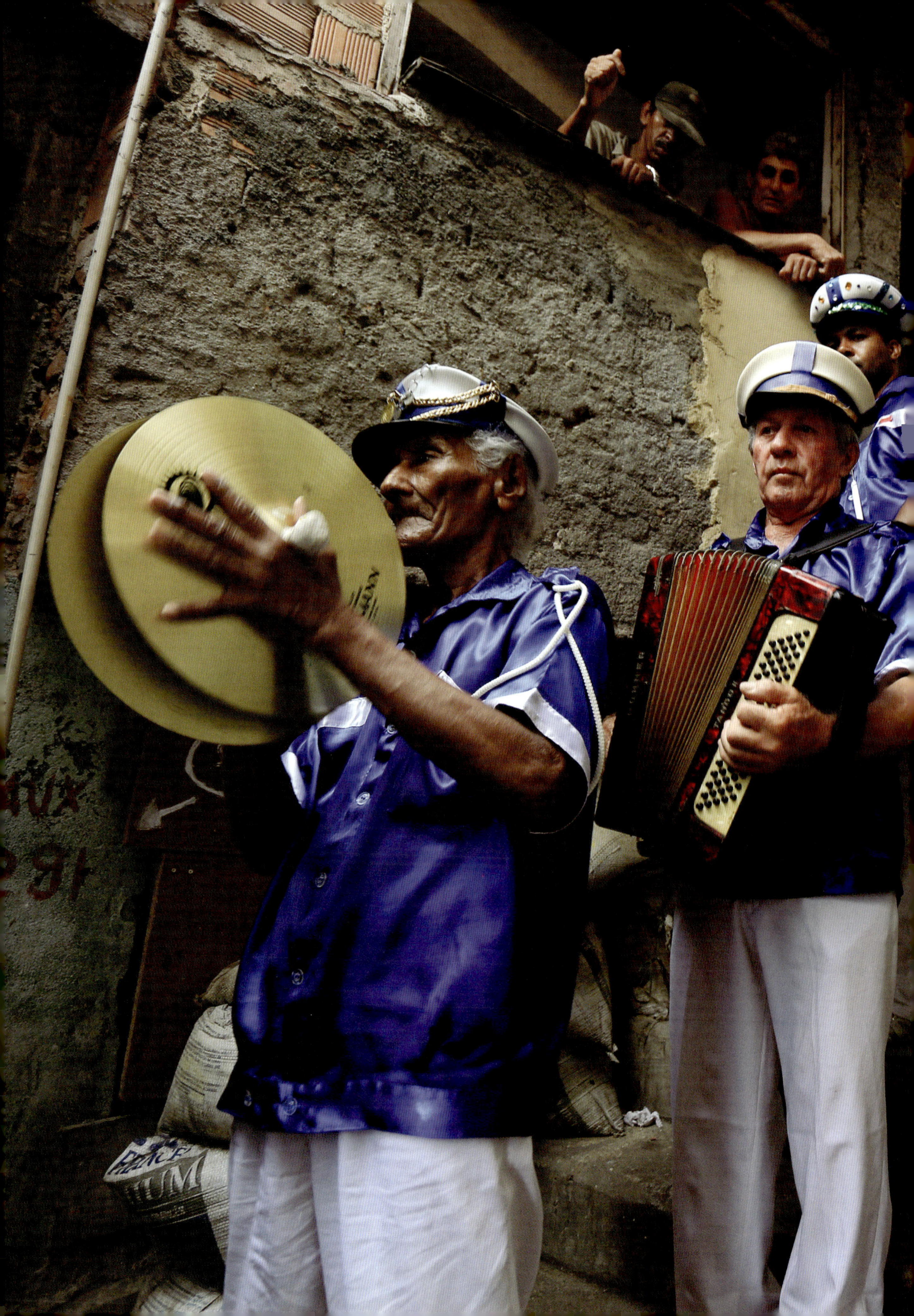

More Music and Celebration

Groups of musicians perform in honor of the Wise Men who visited the Christ Child in Bethlehem. This group journeys through the narrow alleys of Santa Marta, a favela built on a steep hillside in the southern part of Rio de Janeiro.

What do Brazilians do after all the excitement of Christmas and New Year's Eve have ended? Do they relax and unwind? Well—yes, but not for long. In this South American country, the celebrations continue for up to a week after Christmas and New Year's Eve have come and gone.

In early January, for example, some coastal towns hold parades to honor Good Lord Jesus of the Navigators and ask Christ to bless sailors at sea. In another tradition, musical groups sing in honor of the Wise Men who visited the Christ Child. Meanwhile, holiday parades and theater continue to enliven towns with music and dance.

57

Parades and boats

Sailors have long been important in Brazil. Even today, most Brazilians live near the Atlantic coast or along the nation's rivers. The processions in honor of Senhor Bom Jesus dos Navegantes (*say NOOR bohm jheh ZHOOS doos nah vay GAHN tehs—Good Lord Jesus of the Navigators*) reflect this history. The galas ask blessings for those who go to sea and express thanks for that protection. Brazilians appreciate these Roman Catholic ceremonies for their entertainment value as well as their religious significance. The flamboyant parades attract viewers of all ages.

Some towns hold part of their procession on land and part of it on water. The water parades include all sorts of boats—from fireboats to luxury yachts, from sailboats to speedboats. Owners have dressed each vessel for the occasion—festooned with flowers, decorated with banners and Brazilian flags, and often adorned with colored lights. Onlookers crowd the shoreline eager for the best view. They spread out their blankets, break open the cold drinks, and enjoy the parade. The weather is usually ideal for this occasion—bright, hot, and sunny. Children

A procession carries an image of Bom Jesus dos Navegantes from the harbor beach to the Church of Boa Viagem in the city of Salvador in northeastern Brazil. The procession takes place each New Year's Day.

especially enjoy the colorful water parades, with one beautifully decorated boat after another floating leisurely along. Often the boats pass in no order whatsoever—the humble tug sailing proudly next to the elegant yacht. Each one maneuvers at will, finding its own place. For several hours they sail side-by-side, offering up thanks for protection at sea.

To ask for continued blessing and protection in the upcoming year, a Catholic ceremony takes place at the end of the parade. Often, several people carry a statue of the Virgin and Child to church on a platform, accompanied by a cheering and joyful crowd. Many people sing songs and hymns in honor of this very special day for those who sail at sea. When the street procession arrives at the church, the participants carry the statue up to the altar with great ceremony, and a priest blesses it. Worshippers crowd the church. After a special ceremony, some people may linger, singing and dancing in the streets. Others return to their boats and sail home—content in the knowledge that it will be another safe year at sea under holy protection.

A musical journey

Folia de reis (foh LEE ah djee rays) means *Festival of the Kings.* This tradition, which developed in rural areas of Brazil, pays tribute to the *Tres Reis (trays rays*—Three Kings), also known as the Three Wise Men. According to the book of Matthew in the Bible, Wise Men from the East visited the infant Jesus in Bethlehem. They gave the Christ Child gifts of gold, frankincense, and myrrh and then returned to their own lands. The folia de reis is meant to reenact their journey home, spreading blessings and the good news of Jesus's birth.

Groups of musicians make the journey. The groups are called by several names, including folias de reis or *companhias de reis (kohm poh NEE ahs djee rays*—companies of kings). The groups travel from one house to another, performing songs and offering blessings in exchange for gifts of food or money. Traditionally, the gifts pay for a large feast for the whole neighborhood on January 6, the day celebrated as Three Kings' Day. Sometimes, however, a wealthy patron pays for the feast, and the group donates the money to a charity or other organization. Most groups begin their ritual journey on December 24 and end it on January 6. In some regions, groups start a few days earlier or continue a few days longer.

The companhias de reis sing and play with enthusiam and skill. Many of their songs tell about the birth of Christ. Groups compose much of their own music, and they often improvise verses to fit a specific situation. For example, if they visit the home of a sick child, they may improvise verses to bless the child with good health in the new year.

The singers and instrumentalists often wear bright costumes. Sometimes three singers, representing the Three Kings, wear crowns. Most groups include several *palhaços* (*pah LYAH suhs*—clowns). The clowns have the most elaborate costumes, including masks of almost every variety and color. The masks—sometimes scary, sometimes animallike—are almost always the innovative creations of the revelers themselves. Some are simple paper or plastic masks, while others feature elaborate face paint and feathers. As a group travels from house to house, its clowns interact with bystanders—playfully entertaining them, teasing the crowd into joining the parade, or coaxing people to sing and dance with them.

The clowns also have the serious task of protecting the group's *bandeira* (banner). Each group has its own *bandeira dos santos reis* (banner of the Holy Kings). Usually, the banner bears an image of the Holy Family—Mary, Joseph, and the baby Jesus. When people make a donation, sometimes they attach a ribbon or a small picture to the banner.

Before a group starts its journey, it arranges which houses it will visit. On approaching a house, it must ask permission to enter. The group sings what is called The Chant of the Door. According to tradition, only the head of the household may open the door to invite them in, and only after they have finished this song. The banner enters first, followed by the musicians and clowns. The musicians pay their respects before the family's presépio and then sing to the family and bless them. The family,

Folia de reis musicians play several types of guitars, including small ten-string instruments called violas.

Musical Notes

The folias de reis use a wide variety of musical instruments. The most common three are a small, 10-string guitar that Brazilians call a *viola*; a small, double-headed snare drum called a *caixa* (ky SHAH); and a tambourine, or *pandeiro* (pahn DEER oh).

The sweet music of a classical guitar or a Brazilian fiddle, known as a *rabeca,* can be part of the ensemble. Someone may squeeze a lively tune from a *sanfona* (small accordion), beat time on a *zabumba* (bass drum), or enrich the melody with a vertical flute. Maracas and a *reco-reco*, a type of scraper, add musical accents. Other types of popular Brazilian music use many of the same instruments.

Snare drums (above top) and tambourines (directly above) are common instruments in Brazilian music. A reco-reco (below) is a long, grooved scraper that adds to the music's rhythm.

More Music and Celebration

The musicians in this folia de reis dress alike in fairly simple blue uniforms, but the clowns wear wildly imaginative costumes.

in turn, has prepared an abundance of food and drink for the performers to enjoy before heading to their next destination.

Traditionally, most groups visit houses within their own neighborhoods. Larger towns might have several groups crisscrossing them during the holiday season. A few groups travel on horseback or by foot through the countryside to farms or other villages. When they arrive at a village, they are served food that is the specialty of that region or town. The hosts also may serve such Brazilian favorites as *feijoada (FAH zhoh AH dah)* and *churrasco*. Feijoada, the national dish of Brazil, is a stew of black beans with a variety of meats. It usually is eaten with white rice, farofa, kale, and oranges. Churrasco, Brazilian-style barbecue, originated among the gauchos on the country's cattle ranches.

These foods may also be part of a wonderful feast, often an outdoor barbecue, held on Three Kings' Day. The folia members and their families, the families they visited, and other friends and neighbors all gather for the party. The food tastes good. There is music and dancing. It is a great way to end a special journey.

The folia de reis tradition is still most common in rural parts

Christmas Lights Up Brazil

of Brazil. However, some people who have moved from the countryside to the large cities have brought the tradition with them. Other changes have also occurred. Once, only men participated as singers, instrumentalists, or clowns. Today, some groups include women and children, which has influenced the sound of their music.

Festive song and dance

Another popular event in Brazil is a kind of folklore theater known as the *pastoril*. Derived from old Portuguese traditions that celebrated the Nativity, the pastorils today are theatrical presentations that revolve around the *pastoras*, or *shepherdesses*, who have the lead roles. The pastoras sing songs and perform dances that may be either religious or secular in nature. For instance, a dance called "The Seduction" portrays the devil trying unsuccessfully to influence a shepherdess toward evil. Then there are three free-spirited dances known as the "Butterfly Dance," the "Gypsy Woman Dance," and the "Ribbons Dance." The pastoras may also sing a series of lively songs known as the chulas. These folklore productions are colorful, spontaneous, uninhibited. Groups perform them before delighted audiences throughout the holiday season.

Some events held during the Christmas season may also take place at other times of the year, depending on the customs of different towns or cities. Among these events are *congada* processions. Special congada groups made up of brilliantly

Feijoada is a popular black bean stew made with a variety of meats—anything from pork ribs to beef tongue, separately or in combination. Feijoada completa (feijoada complete) also includes the traditional side dishes— white rice, farofa, kale, and oranges.

More Music and Celebration

Colorfully dressed groups perform as a congada procession makes its way along a street strung with red and white banners.

costumed singers, dancers, and musicians perform in these flamboyant parades.

The congada tradition reflects a combination of African and European influences. It grew out of the European tradition of religious processions and plays. Congadas are often staged in honor of the patron saint of a city or church and include a Roman Catholic religious service. Through song and dance, the performers also tell a dramatic story that features a mock battle and a royal coronation at the court of an African king and queen. African culture strongly influences the style of dance. Even people who don't actively join in the dance parade have fun watching it from the sidelines. The congada is an exotic and playful affair—the kind of lively religious festival that is typical of Brazil.

Another popular festivity that may be held in the Christmas season or at other times of the year is the *Bumba-meu-boi*.

This theatrical event takes place throughout the country and is especially elaborate in the Northeast. Its music and dance blend African, Native American, and Portuguese influences.

The Bumba-meu-boi is a story about a *boi*, or ox. There are many variations of the story, depending on the region in which it is performed. In one version, the ox, who dances and leaps among the audience, is killed by a gaucho to prepare a meal for his wife. When the cattle owner discovers that his animal is missing, he demands that the gaucho produce it, threatening to kill the gaucho if he does not return the ox. A folk doctor revives the ox and saves the gaucho's life.

The play incorporates music, rhyme, and dance and can last for several hours. Costumes may be extremely elaborate. The ox costume often consists of wood, wire, and cloth. Velvet or flowery cotton covers a mesh foundation. The head is usually made of painted papier-mâché, with flowers or ribbons adorning the horns.

It's a Bumba-meu-boi! In this play, the ox wears the fanciest costume.

One season ends, another begins

With the arrival of Three Kings' Day on January 6, the Christmas season in Brazil comes to an end. Businesses close in observance of this holy day, also known as Epiphany, which commemorates the visit of the Wise Men to the holy infant Jesus. Some families still follow an old Portuguese custom on the eve of Epiphany. The children put their shoes beside the window or outside the door, hoping to find them filled with treats in the morning. Usually, they are not disappointed. Tradition says it is the Three Kings who fill the shoes with goodies, although parents might provide a little help. Either way, on the morning of January 6, children find their shoes filled with chocolates and other goodies—a fitting end to the Christmas season.

Three Kings' Day is also the time when many Brazilians put away their Christmas trees and presépios. City workers take down street decorations. Shopping malls and boutiques replace their Christmas displays with something new. There are no more end-of-the-year celebrations, no more special Christmas observances to keep, and no more rowdy pastorils.

This does not mean, however, that the festivities in Brazil have ended. On the contrary, now that the Christmas season is over, there is only one thing for Brazilians to do: start preparing for the next big celebration—Carnival.

While Christmas marks the beginning of Brazil's summer festivities, Carnival brings them to a glorious conclusion. It is an exuberant celebration that immediately precedes Lent, the religious season set aside in the Christian church's calendar for spiritual renewal and devotion in preparation for Easter. Brazil's multiday Carnival is famous the world over for the sheer size and extravagance of its street parades, costumes, and balls—to say nothing of the nonstop singing and dancing. Although it won't take place until February or early March, Carnival is a perfect way to end the summer season, and it gives everyone something to look forward to now that Christmas is over. And in Brazil, everyone needs at least one more festival to look forward to. After all, what is life without a celebration?

This tile mosaic of the Three Kings worshipping the Christ Child comes from the Nossa do Rosário dos Pretos Church, built by African-Brazilians in the 1700's. The church stands in the historic center of Salvador.

Christmas Lights Up Brazil

Crafts

An "Eggcellent" Wreath

Brighten up a door or wall with a colorful wreath made from egg cartons.

Materials
- pencil
- ruler
- foam board
- scissors
- acrylic paint in multiple colors, such as green, yellow, orange, blue, and purple
- paint brushes
- 3 to 5 egg cartons made from paper
- hot glue gun*
- heavy monofilament fishing line

* adult supervision is needed

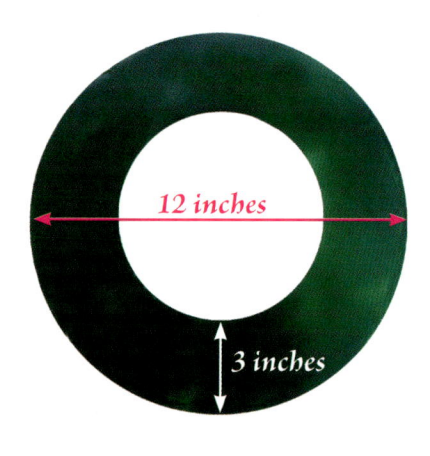

1. Cut a ring 12 inches (30 cm) in diameter and 3 inches (8 cm) wide from the foam board. Following the directions on the paint bottle, cover the entire ring with green paint, and allow to dry.

2. Cut out different sized leaf shapes, similar to those shown here, from the top of the egg carton. Paint both sides green, and allow to dry. A minimum of 20 leaves will be needed.

3. Hot glue single leaves and leaf pairs around the wreath, similar to what is shown. More leaves can be made and added if desired.

4. Cut a length of fishing line to use for a hanger. Tie it around the top of the green ring.

5. Using the red lines as a guide, cut apart the egg cartons to separate the cups from the spacers.

The four-cornered shapes will be used for the bottom layer of the flower.

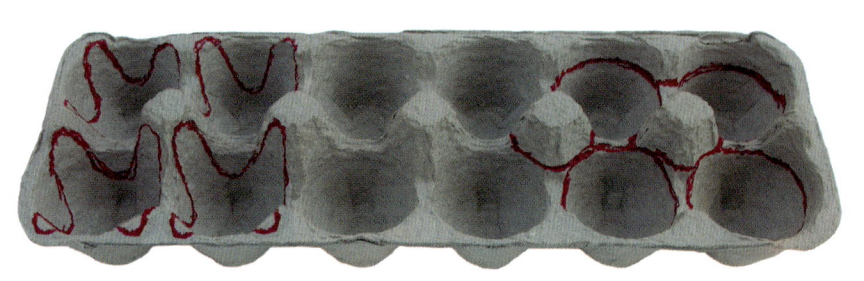

The round shapes will be scalloped and fringed.

68 Christmas Lights Up Brazil

6. Scallop and fringe the cups and spacers similar to the patterns shown here.

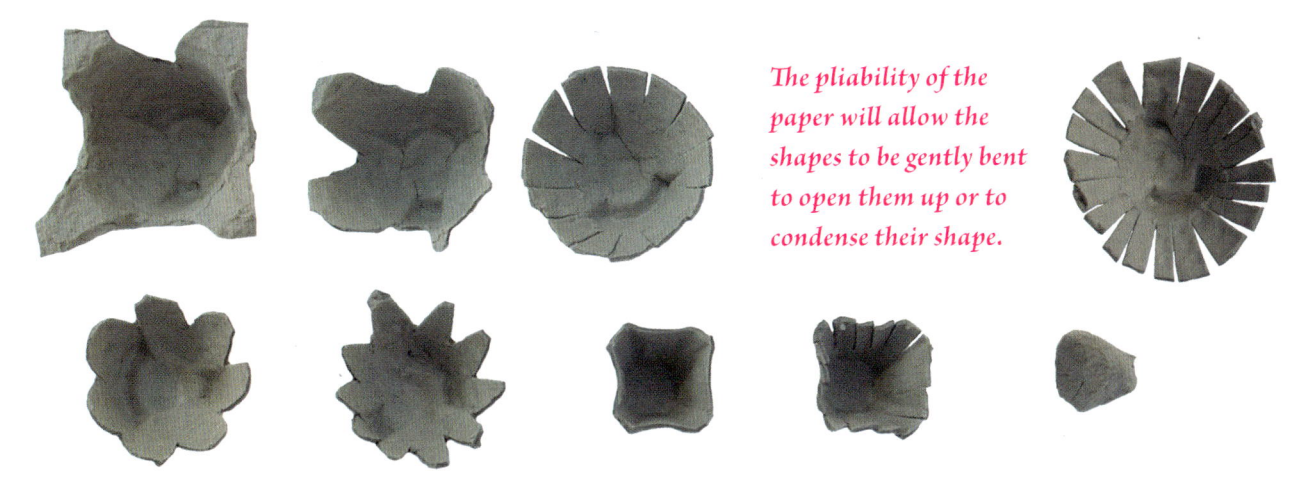

The pliability of the paper will allow the shapes to be gently bent to open them up or to condense their shape.

7. Paint the shapes different colors, and allow to dry.

8. Assemble flowers by layering the different colors and shapes. Hot glue the layers together. Multiple variations can be created, as in these samples.

9. Finally, arrange the flowers on the ring so that they fit snugly together. Hot glue each one to the ring.

Crafts

Festive Globes

Turn a clear glass ornament into swirling festive shapes that will be sure to brighten up your Christmas tree.

1. Take the top off an ornament. Pour in some paint and start turning the ornament. The paint will slowly move and form patterns.

   The paint can be thinned with a few drops of water. However, if the paint is too thin, the colors will melt together.

2. Repeat this step with other colors. As the paint dries, it will continue to move.

3. When the paint is completly dry, put the top back in the ornament. Attach a ribbon, if desired, to form a hanger.

Materials
- acrylic paint in multiple colors, such as green, yellow, orange, blue, and purple
- clear glass ornaments
- ribbon
- glue
- glitter

You can partially paint the inside of the ornament so that you can see through the glass. Gluing glitter to a partially painted globe will add an additional sparkle.

Christmas Lights Up Brazil

Recipes

Roast Turkey Brazilian Style (Peru á Brasileira), with dressing

1 turkey (about 14 lbs.), cleaned
¼ tsp. black pepper
1 tsp. salt
3 garlic cloves, pounded to a paste
2 cups white wine
1 chopped onion
1 grated carrot
1 cup vinegar
½ cup celery
½ cup chopped parsley

One day before serving, remove and set aside the gizzard, heart, and liver. Rinse the turkey twice with cold water. Dry out the cavity with paper towels. Pull the neck out of the skin, keeping the skin intact to hold the neck dressing. Prepare marinade by mixing the pepper, ½ teaspoon salt, garlic, wine, onion, carrot, and vinegar together. Soak turkey in marinade overnight, turning occasionally.

The next day, cut the gizzard in half. Rinse under cold water to remove all the stones. Wash the rest of the giblets and cover with 4 cups of water, ½ teaspoon salt, celery, and parsley. Simmer until the giblets are thoroughly cooked. Remove from broth, chop fine, and reserve the liquid. Divide the giblets into two portions, one for each stuffing recipe.

Prepare neck and breast stuffing (see page 72). After neck stuffing cools, stuff the neck and sew the neck skin together. Stuff breast cavity and close and truss the turkey. Bake leftover stuffing separately in a bowl.

Brush turkey well with melted butter and with a mixture of white wine and giblet broth. Roast turkey in oven according to cooking directions supplied with the turkey. Serves about 14.

Neck Stuffing for Roast Turkey (Farofa stuffing)

4 cups manioc meal*
2 tbsp. butter
1 chopped onion
½ cup chopped tomatoes (optional)
¼ cup chopped parsley
1 portion of the reserved giblets
4 or 5 drops Tabasco™ sauce
3 tbsp. butter
1 cup giblet broth
½ cup stuffed olives
3 chopped hard-boiled eggs

Gently brown manioc meal in the oven. Melt 2 tablespoons butter in a large skillet and sauté the onion, tomatoes, and parsley. Add giblets, Tabasco sauce, and the other 3 tablespoons of butter. When butter is melted, remove skillet from heat and gradually stir in the browned manioc meal. Add giblet broth. Mix well until fully blended, then return to low heat, stirring constantly until mixture is loose. Add olives and chopped eggs. Stuff neck cavity of turkey (see turkey recipe, page 71).

*Manioc meal, which is coarser than manioc flour, can be purchased at specialty stores that carry ingredients for cooking Latin American foods. If unavailable, Cream of Wheat™ or Farina™ may be substituted.

Breast Stuffing for Roast Turkey (Bread stuffing)

¼ cup chopped bacon
½ cup chopped onion
¼ cup minced parsley
2 cloves of garlic, minced
½ cup chopped tomatoes
1 cup giblet broth
1 portion of the reserved giblets
6 cups of bread cubes soaked in ¾ cup of milk

Fry bacon in skillet and remove the fat. Add onion, parsley, garlic, and tomatoes. When browned, cover with broth and bring to a boil. Press through a sieve and add giblets and bread. Mix well with a fork. Season to taste. Stuff breast cavity of turkey (see turkey recipe, page 71).

Grilled Pineapple

1 pineapple, with skin and core removed
½ cup brown sugar
2 tsp. cinnamon
Optional: vanilla ice cream or yogurt

Mix brown sugar and cinnamon in a shallow dish. Cut pineapple into ¾ inch slices. Dredge each slice in the sugar mixture, lightly coating both sides. The slices can be refrigerated for up to 30 minutes before cooking.

On an outdoor grill: Brush the grill with vegetable oil. Grill pineapple slices over preheated coals for about 3 to 4 minutes on each side.

To cook indoors: Spray a heavy grill pan with nonstick cooking spray. Grill pineapple slices on top of the stove for 3 to 4 minutes on each side.

Serve alone as a side dish. Serve with ice cream or yogurt for a great light dessert. Serves 4 to 8.

Black Bean Salad

One 15-oz. can black beans, drained and rinsed
1 cup fresh or frozen yellow corn kernels, cooked and drained
1 pint cherry or grape tomatoes, diced
One 14-oz. can hearts of palm, diced
½ cup orange bell pepper, cored and diced
¼ cup diced red onion
¼ cup thinly sliced scallions (include some of the green)
½ cup minced fresh cilantro leaves

Vinaigrette Dressing
2 tbsp. sherry vinegar
1 tbsp. lime juice
½ tsp. ground cumin
¼ tsp. salt
freshly ground black pepper to taste
pinch sugar
⅓ cup olive oil

In a large bowl, mix together beans, corn, tomatoes, hearts of palm, bell pepper, onion, scallions, and cilantro.

In a small bowl, whisk together vinegar, lime juice, cumin, salt, pepper, and sugar until combined. Add the oil in a stream, whisking, and whisk the dressing until it is emulsified. Pour the dressing over the bean mixture and toss to combine. Refrigerate until ready to serve, at least one hour.

Salad may be served with a sliced avocado and lime wedges on the side. Serves 6.

Lentil Soup (Sopa de lentilha)

2 tbsp. olive oil
2 slices bacon, cut in small pieces
3 carrots, peeled and diced
1 stalk of celery, diced (about ½ cup)
1 shallot (or small onion), diced
4 cups beef broth
1 cup water

One 14-oz. can of diced tomatoes in sauce
1 large potato, cubed
½ cup finely chopped spinach or kale (fresh or frozen)
1 cup lentils
¾ tsp. oregano

Pour 2 tablespoons of olive oil into a large, heavy pot. Sauté the bacon, carrots, celery, and shallot until the shallot is soft and translucent. Add broth, water, tomatoes, potato, spinach, lentils, and oregano. Bring the liquid to a boil, then immediately turn down heat and simmer at medium-low temperature for about 45 minutes to an hour. Serves 6 to 8.

Recipes

Rabanada

8 slices French bread
1 cup light cream (half and half)
½ tsp. vanilla
¼ tsp. salt
1 tbsp. sugar
2 eggs

½ cup sugar (for coating)
1 tbsp. cinnamon

Garnish:
Fresh fruits, such as strawberries and bananas, make a pretty—and tasty—garnish.

Let bread sit out overnight to get a little stale. Slice bread into pieces about ½ to ¾ inch thick. Arrange the slices in a large casserole dish.

Whisk together cream, vanilla, salt, and 1 tablespoon of sugar. Pour mixture over bread slices. Refrigerate for about 20 minutes, turning slices over halfway through the time. Mix sugar and cinnamon for the coating in a shallow bowl, and set aside.

Whisk eggs in another shallow bowl. Spray a large frying pan with nonstick cooking spray, and preheat the pan over medium heat. Dip each piece of bread in the eggs, turning it over to coat both sides. Handle the bread gently, since it is already soft. Fry bread on both sides until golden brown. Dip each bread slice in the sugar mixture, generously coating all sides. Serve warm. Serves 4 to 8.

Coconut Carrot Muffins

1 cup flour
½ tsp. baking powder
½ tsp. baking soda
¼ tsp. salt
½ tsp. cinnamon
¼ tsp. nutmeg
small dash of cloves
½ cup chopped pecans
½ cup grated unsweetened coconut
1 cup finely shredded carrots
    (about 2-3 large carrots)

2 tbsp. vanilla yogurt
6 tbsp. melted butter
2 eggs
⅓ cup brown sugar
⅓ cup white sugar
½ cup raisins

Variation:
For mini muffins, substitute ¼ cup finely ground pecans for the chopped pecans.

Preheat oven to 350 °F (175 °C).

    Combine flour, baking powder, baking soda, salt, and the spices in a large bowl. Add the ground pecans and coconut. Wash, peel, and shred the carrots, and put them in another bowl. Mix the yogurt with the carrots. Melt butter in a small saucepan over low heat.

    Whisk together the eggs and sugars for about 1 minute. Stir in the carrot mixture. Add the melted butter. Pour the liquids into the flour mixture, and stir just until blended. Add raisins.

    Spray 12 medium-sized muffin pan cups or 24 mini muffin pan cups with nonstick baking spray. Spoon batter evenly into muffin cups.

    Bake about 20 to 25 minutes (15 to 20 minutes for mini muffins). Serve plain or with whipped cream cheese.

Recipes

Pineapple Coconut Smoothie

1 cup coconut milk
1 ½ cups fresh pineapple chunks
½ cup sweetened condensed milk
1 tbsp. freshly squeezed lime juice
2 lime slices

Cut a lime in half. To make garnish, cut two lime slices and then cut the center of each half-slice partway to the peel. Squeeze the remaining lime to obtain 1 tablespoon of juice.

    In a blender, combine coconut milk, pineapple, sweetened condensed milk, and lime juice. Pour into glasses over crushed ice. Hang a lime slice on the rim of each glass. Serves two.

Pinch of Guava (Beliscão de goiabada) Cookies

6 tbsp. butter, plus some to spread
½ cup sugar
½ cup media crema (or vanilla yogurt)*
1 ¾ cups flour
guava jam or fruit spread
3 tbsp. finely ground pecans
4 tbsp. granulated sugar
1 egg white, lightly beaten

Cream 6 tablespoons butter and ½ cup sugar. Add media crema (or vanilla yogurt). Blend in flour. Knead dough together by hand to form 3 or 4 balls. Refrigerate about 3 hours.

    Roll out a section of dough about halfway. Gently spread it with a thin layer of soft butter. Fold it in half and in half again, and pinch the sides together. Roll out to about ⅛ inch (0.3 cm) thick. Cut dough into circles 2 ½ inches (6 cm) in diameter. Put ½ teaspoon of guava jam in the center of each circle. Lift two opposite sides of the circle toward each other and pinch them together over the filling. Mix 4 tablespoons of sugar with the ground pecans. Brush each cookie with egg white and sprinkle it with a small amount of the sugar mixture. Bake on ungreased cookie sheets at 350 °F (175 °C) for about 15 minutes. Remove from cookie sheets, and cool on wire racks. Makes 4 to 5 dozen cookies.

*Media crema is a canned cream that has a consistency similar to yogurt. In the United States, it is available in some grocery stores and Latin American specialty food stores. As a substitute, use ½ cup vanilla yogurt.

Lullaby for Baby Jesus
Repousa tranquilo O meigo Jesus

Translated from the Portuguese
English version by R.H.

Brazilian
Arranged by R.H.

Tenderly and smoothly

1. Sleep qui-et-ly, my Jesus, Now close Thy dear eyes. A-bove Thee shine God's count-less stars, Like dia-monds in the sky. Be-side Thy bed, a man-ger crude, Where cat-tle have fed, Thy Moth-er stands in watch-ful prayer, And strokes Thy bless-ed head.

2. The shep-herds leave their flocks and come, They bring Thee their love, While an-gels of our Fath'r in heav'n Re-joice in song a-bove. From far a-way the Wise Men three Their treas-ures do bring. The whole wide world be-fore Thee kneels, My Je-sus, lit-tle King.

Carols

Away in a Manger
Na Manjedoura

Letra atribuída a Martinho Lutero, 1535
Mel. atribuída a Martinho Lutero, 1530
Trad. de Adelina Cerqueira Leite, 1947

Andante

1. Sem lar e sem berço, deitado em capim,
Os braços movendo, Jesus chama assim.
Estrelas abrindo as cortinas dos céus
Espiam na gruta o Menino que é Deus.

2. O gado mugindo, põe-se Êle a sorrir,
A nós prenunciando um alegre porvir!
Eu te amo, Jesus; vem meu sono velar
E fica ao meu lado até o dia clarear.

3. Conduz os meus passos na trilha do bem
E teu amor dá-me, eu te peço também.
Vigia as crianças, prepara o seu lar
Nos céus onde irão junto a Ti habitar.

From *Cânticos do Natal,* selected and annotated by Henriqueta Rosa Fernandes Braga, © 1954

Silent Night
Noite de paz!

José Mohr, 1818
Adapt. da Comissão do Hinário,* 1945

Francisco Xavier Gruber, 1818

Andante

1. Noi-te de paz! Noi-te de amor! Tu-do dor-me em, der-re-dor.
En-tre os as-tros que es- par-gem a luz, Pro-cla-man-do o Me-ni-no Je-sus,
Bri-lha a es-tre-la da paz! Bri-lha a es-tre-la da paz!

2. Noite de paz! Noite de amor!
   Nas campinas ao pastor,
   Lindos anjos, mandados por Deus,
   Anunciam a nova dos céus —
   Nasce o bom Salvador,
   Nasce o bom Salvador.

3. Noite de paz! Noite de amor!
   Oh! Que belo resplendor
   Ilumina o Menino Jesus!
   No presépio do mundo eis a luz,
   Sol de eterno fulgor!
   Sol de eterno fulgor!

*Por gentileza da Confederação Evangélica do Brasil.
From *Cânticos do Natal,* selected and annotated by Henriqueta Rosa Fernandes Braga, © 1954

Acknowledgments

Cover	© Dabldy/iStockphoto	42	© T photography/Shutterstock
3	© Paulo Nabas, Shutterstock	43	© Maria Adelaide Silva, Alamy Images
5	© Filipe Frazao, Shutterstock	44	© Shutterstock; © Africa Studio/Shutterstock
6	© A. Ricardo, Shutterstock	45	© Shutterstock
8	© SJ Travel Photo and Video/Shutterstock	46	© Dreamstime
10	Grandes Personagens da Nossa História; © Godong/Alamy Images	49	© Fernanda Paradizo, Shutterstock
11	WORLD BOOK map	50	© Joa Souza, iStockphoto
12	© Celso Diniz, Shutterstock	51	© Shutterstock; © Joa Souza, Shutterstock
13	© Dlrz4114/Dreamstime	53	© Rune Landale, iStockphoto
14	© Marchello74/Shutterstock	54	© Andre Luiz Moreira, Shutterstock
16	© iStockphoto	55	© Dreamstime; © Vanderlei Almeida, AFP/Getty Images
18	© P&R Fotos/age fotostock/SuperStock	56	© Ratao Diniz, Brazil Photos/Getty Images
19	© Levi Bianco, Getty Images	58	© Yasuyoshi Chiba, AFP/Getty Images
20	© Alexandre Fagundes De Fagundes, Dreamstime	61	© Igor Alecsander, iStockphoto; © Elena Fragoso, Shutterstock; © Carlos Pinheiro, Dreamstime; © Su Justen, Shutterstock
21	© Yasuyoshi Chiba, AFP/Getty Images		
22	© Dreamstime	62	© Igor Alecsander, iStockphoto
23	© R.M. Nunes, Shutterstock	63	© Shutterstock
24	© Igor Alecsander, iStockphoto	64	© Nilton Cardin, Getty Images
26	© Fabio Teixeira, AFP/Getty Images	65	© Universal Images Group North America LLC/DeAgostini/Alamy Images
28	© A. Einsiedler, Shutterstock		
29	© Look Die Bildagentur der Fotografen GmbH/Alamy Images	66	© Godong/Alamy Images
30	© Lilyana Vynogradova, Shutterstock	67-70	WORLD BOOK photos by Brenda Tropinski
32	© age fotostock/Alamy Images	71	© Tina Fields, iStockphoto
35	© Carla Nichiata, Shutterstock; © Angela Aladro mella, Shutterstock	73	© Nataliya Arzamasova, Shutterstock
36	© Iuliia Timofeeva, Shutterstock	74	© Carla Nichiata, Shutterstock
37	© Orlando Kissner, AFP/Getty Images	75	© Bernashafo/Shutterstock
39	© iStockphoto	76	© AS Food studio/Shutterstock
40	© Dreamstime		
41	© Yasuyoshi Chiba, AFP/Getty Images		

Christmas Lights Up Brazil

Prospect Heights Public Library
12 N. Elm Street
Prospect Heights, IL 60070
www.phpl.info